CAN YOU GUESS
WHO'S COMING TO DINNER

A Special Christmas Surprise

Scripture Reference: Tyndale NLT

ISBN-13:978-1503114913   ISBN-10:1503114910

Christmas Is Coming

I want to have a party
and invite all of my old friends.

I know,

A Christmas Eve Party!

A great big

Dinner party

But I'm going to need a lot of help to contact all of my old friends.

Who can I get to help me find all of my old friends?

I know just the person who can help.

I'll write a letter to Santa and see if he can get Mrs. Claus and the elves to help locate my friends and invite them to my dinner party. If anyone knows where they all are; He does.

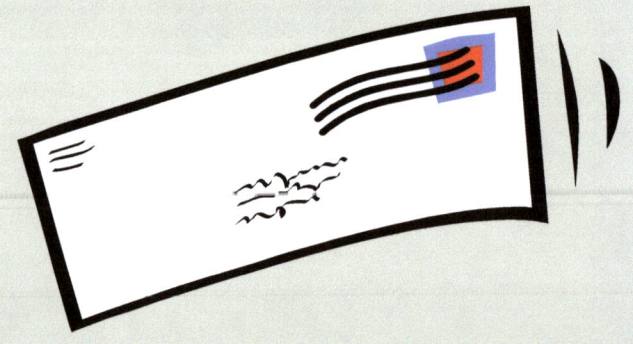

Lou Carol Franklin
777 Blessed Street
Syracuse, NY 13200

Yeah!

YEAH!

Santa answered my letter. He and Mrs. Claus thought the dinner party was a great ideal.   He said the elves have already started to contact all my old friends and they will all be here on Christmas Eve for the special dinner party.

I am so excited!
Santa and Mrs. Claus
are going to help me
have the best
Christmas ever!

We'll start getting everything ready

The decorations are up

It's Time! My Guest Are Starting To Come.

We have lots of food
and cookies to eat
candy, cakes, and
yummy Christmas
Treats

Guess Who's Coming To Dinner

Hi everyone,

what a fun party

Merry Christmas

Hi, Merry Christmas everybody, we're Berry happy to be here, thanks for inviting us.

Frosty's here!
He has to stay outside,
But I'm so glad
he came.

Thanks for coming Drummer Boy

Glad you came Mr. Nutcracker

The Three Kings Are Here

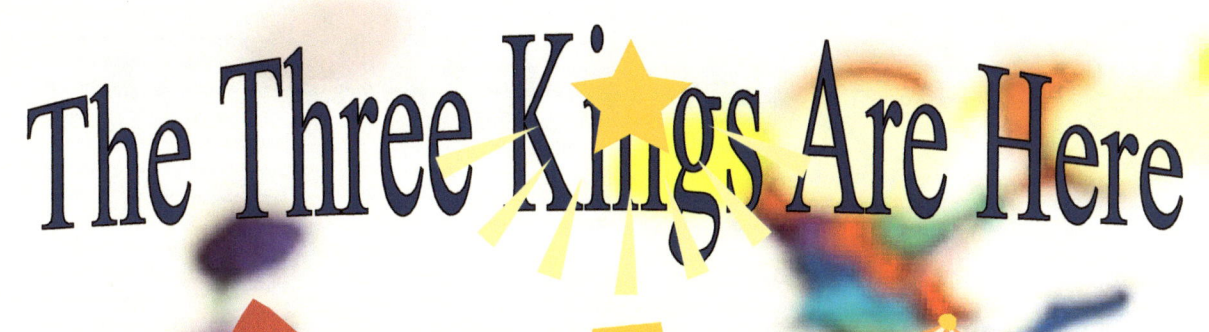

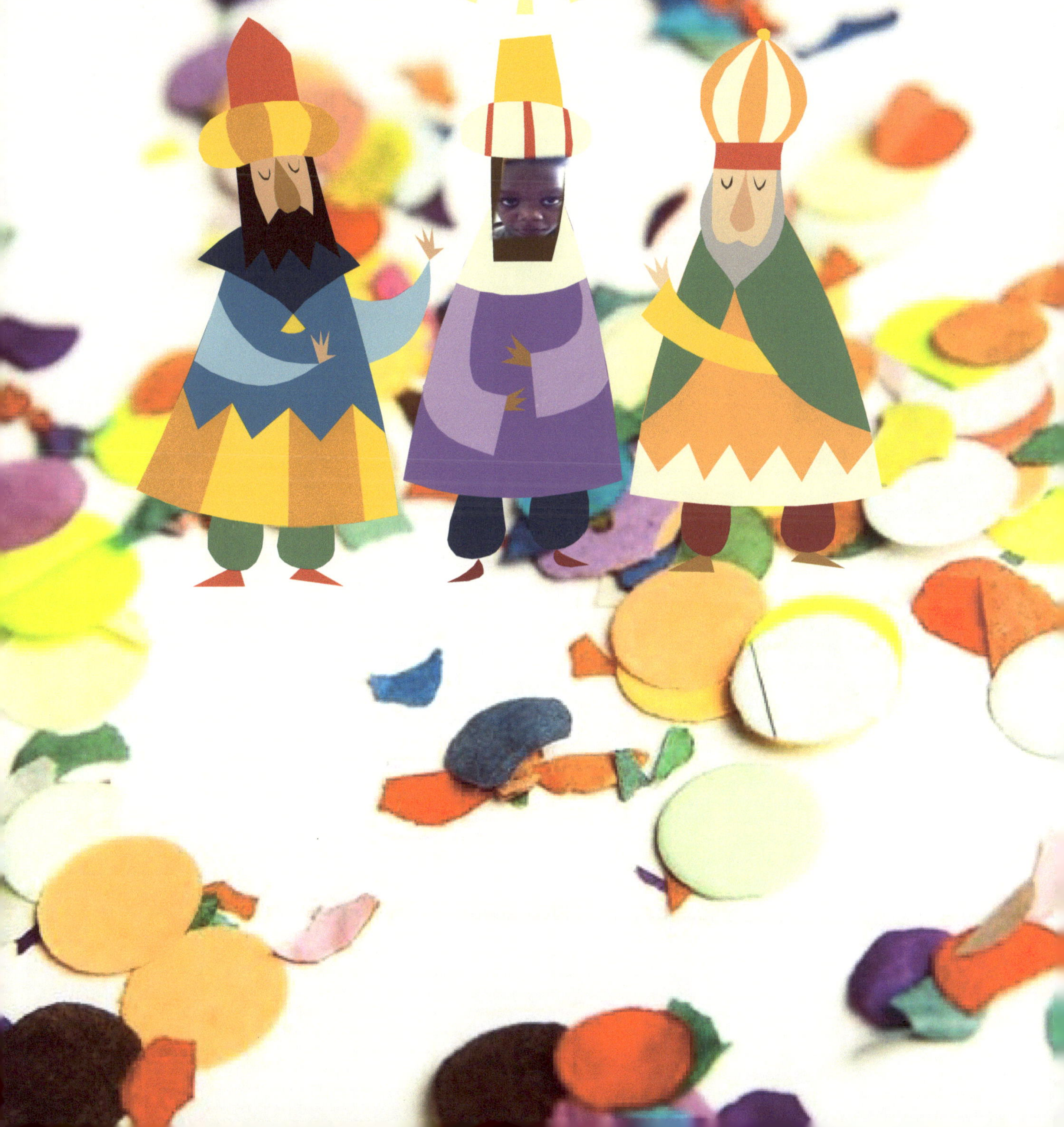

The Shepherds are here

Merry Christmas Everyone.
Everybody's here except for
two more people and I know
they'll be here soon.

I see Santa's reindeer outside

Hey Everybody, Santa's Here!

Thank you Santa for getting all of my old friends to come to my party.

You, Mrs. Claus and the elves did a great job!

Now I have a surprise for you Santa, I invited one more very special guest, and they should be here soon, can you

Guess Who's Coming To Dinner?

Let's Sing A Christmas Carol

♪

Joy to the World

The Lord has come

Let earth recieve her King

Knock, Knock, Knock

He's Here!
My Special Guest is Here!

Merry Christmas Everybody!

Can You Guess

Who's Coming To Dinner?

Come on everybody

Let's go open the door!

O Holy Night
The Stars are Brightly Shining

I'm here knocking
if you open
I'll come in and eat with you.

Look! I stand at the door and knock,
if you hear my voice and open the door,
I will come in, and we will share a meal together as friends.

Revelation 3:20 NLT

Merry Christmas

www.ingramcontent.com/pod-product-compliance
Lightning Source LLC
Chambersburg PA
CBHW041525280526
45792CB00004B/1391